WELCOME TO MY LIFE OF DOOM!

By Kerri Lane

Illustrated by Jeremy Ley

Pearson Australia
(a division of Pearson Australia Group Pty Ltd)
707 Collins Street, Melbourne, Victoria 3008
PO Box 23360, Melbourne, Victoria 8012
www.pearson.com.au

First published 2012 by Pearson Australia
2019 2018 2017 2016
10 9 8 7 6 5 4 3 2

Commissioning Editor: Sabine Bolick
Project Editor: Suzy Freeman
Editor: Sophie Ayerbe
Designer: Nina Heryanto
Copyright & Pictures Editor: Marg Barber
Illustrator: Jeremy Ley
Printed in Australia by the SOS Print + Media Group

ISBN 978 1 4425 3778 1

Pearson Australia Group Pty Ltd ABN 40 004 245 943

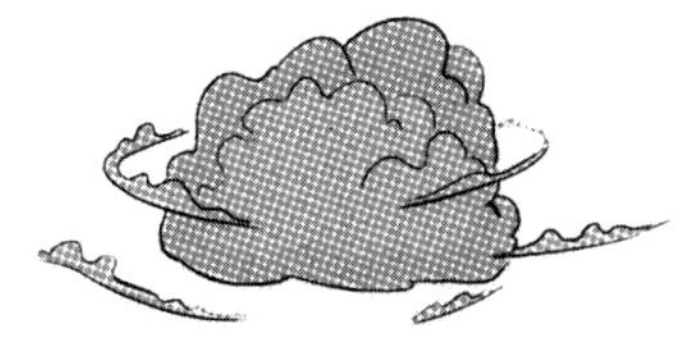

CONTENTS

Chapter 1 

Doomsville

The TV remote went sailing through the air. Pride puffed up my chest. I was watching sheer poetry in motion. Perfect curve. Sizzling top spin. And headed straight for…

"Catch it!" I yelled frantically. "Quick!"

My sister's fingers wriggled about like slippery worms. "I can't! Oops, I…"

A crashing sound filled the air. Bits of splintered glass from the TV screen flew in all directions like mini torpedoes. I dived behind the lounge, and when I dared to lift my head, there was silence. Mum and Dad ran into the room and looked at me in shock, their mouths hanging open like Venus flytraps.

Unfortunately, the silence didn't last. Dad's face suddenly went from shocked white to raging purple. "Matthew! You are banned from watching the other TV, and from using the computer, too!"

"But Dad! It wasn't my faul—"

Dad's expression blocked my argument. "Until you're ninety, Matthew! Got it?"

No TV? "But the Jets game starts in an hour!" I glanced over at Mum, but she looked even angrier than Dad. The Jets were the best basketball team in the world.

"Dustpan and brush! Now!" she ordered.

I couldn't believe this was happening six days before my birthday! And just because my sister couldn't catch. Is it my fault I have the power of a fast bowler? Some parents would be proud to have an almost eleven-year-old son who could put top spin on a ball—or remote control—with such skill.

Back in my room, I flopped onto my bed and weighed up my options. I had to face facts.

I live in the house of **doom**. If anything bad is going to happen, it'll happen to me.

Okay, maybe that means I live under the cloud of doom. Because come to think of it, I go to the school of doom as well. So, maybe the **doom** follows me wherever I go!

That would explain a lot. Like how my homework suddenly disappeared out of my schoolbag. Let's face it—I'm even the fan of doom. That's why the Jets have lost their last five home games. If I'm there, they lose! If I watch them live on TV, they lose!

So, there I was, lying in misery on the bed of doom, in the room of doom, in the house of **doom**.

Welcome to my life.

Idly, I bounced a ping-pong ball against the wall. And sighed again. And tried to work out how to get seventy-nine years, six days and twenty-three hours shaved off my sentence.

In my mind it was do-able. It wasn't like the TV had been new.

And hadn't I already suffered cruelly for a whole hour and a half! "I wonder whether the Jets will still be around when I'm ninety, because that's probably the next time I'll get to see them!" I muttered.

That depressed me even more, so I scanned the room for something to take my mind off all my troubles. Hockey gear. That could do it. It wouldn't be long till the season began, so maybe I should test out my new stick.

I kitted up. Then I picked up the stick. I gave a few swings to test the weight again. Light as a feather. Sweet. I didn't have a ball, so I lined up a few old stuffed toys that Mum wouldn't let me throw away, and aimed and fired. **Bad move...**

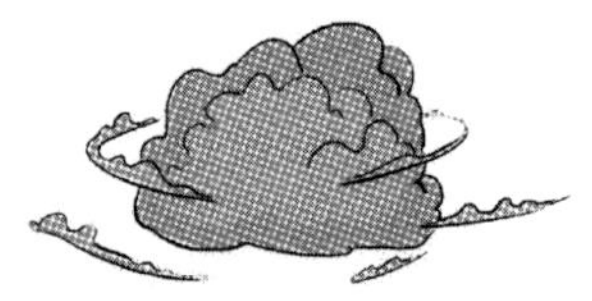

Chapter 2 

Strike Two

"Yes! Ted the Bear hits the back of the net!" (Also known as the bedroom door.) I lined up Cougar the Cat and swung again. "Yes! Another score from Matt the Marvel!"

Beanbag Bill was next. Now this little guy could fly. He's got the weight, which means he'll have speed. This was the big one.

I stood back against the window and started my run. And continued my commentary. "Matthew Kronberg weaves around the chair, sidesteps the desk, hurdles the schoolbag and deftly avoids an attack from the cupboard!

"Curling his body in tight, he reaches forward, hooks Beanbag Bill and lifts him with all his might and skill. BB Bill sails through the air! Listen to that crowd cheer! Kronberg lifts his arms in victory! Matt the Marvel is doing it ag—"

"Ahhh! What…?"

"Mum! Are you okay?" I dropped the hockey stick and ran to her, instantly feeling a teeny bit better when she was still standing and I couldn't see any blood. "Mum! Why didn't you knock? Especially when there could be a game in play!"

All I could see of Mum's face were her eyes. Both her hands covered her nose and lower face.

Those eyes were growing wider. And they glared like lightning rods.

"Mum? Say something! Are you really hurt? Are you okay?"

"Matthew Kronberg," she said in this funny nasally voice, "I'm going to find you something else in life besides sport, if it's the last thing I do!"

"But Mum! It was an accident, truly! I'm really sorry! I didn't mean it..."

She was shaking her head. "Tomorrow, Matthew. Your new life starts tomorrow. Be ready for it."

As she walked away, still holding her nose, I was deep in thought. She couldn't mean it, right? But even if she did, she said I'd have a "new life". Right?

That couldn't be so bad. I mean, that would mean my prison sentence was over, wouldn't it, because my prison sentence is part of my "old life"?

And she wouldn't really take away all my sport stuff because sport was good for you, right? Sport keeps you fit and your mind alert.

Well, then why was it feeling like that cloud of **doom** had just settled a bit closer? And like it was ready to rain more bad luck down all over me? It didn't matter how hard I tried, I couldn't shake that feeling.

Chapter 3

TUFF'n'UP

The next day, I didn't know whether to be excited or nervous. I crept down to the kitchen, mixed up some instant porridge and added honey, all the while keeping one eye on the door. When Mum appeared she was holding a package. And wearing a scary smile.

"Been shopping, Mum? Bit early for a Saturday, isn't it?" I asked, trying to lighten the mood a bit.

It didn't work; the scary smile got wider, and scarier. "It's never too early to start a new life, Matthew."

I gulped. "Um, Mum—about this new life..."

Gathering her bag, she tucked the mysterious package under her arm.

"No time to chat now! Come on, we're late for our appointment." She took a quick glance at her watch and then headed out towards the car. I had no choice but to follow.

And all the way that cloud of **doom** kept slipping lower and closer.

In the car, we were silent until we pulled up in front of a building with the words

written in big letters across the front doors. My mood lifted immediately.

"Boxing! Yeah! I've always wanted to try boxing. You're the best Mum!"

I pulled my fists up under my chin and threw out of couple of air jabs, my feet twitched—I couldn't wait!

"Is that what's in the parcel? Boxing gloves?"

This was great!

The only problem was Mum. I thought she'd be really pleased by my reaction to the "new life" she'd chosen, but she wasn't saying a word. Still, I bounded from the car and headed for the door. Just as I began to push it open, she called me back.

And my heart sank. The scary smile was back. "This is our door, Matthew."

She pointed to a little black door I hadn't noticed. It had words on the front, but I couldn't read them properly because Mum was blocking them and pointing to a long, dark flight of stairs. All I caught was a name: Madame Cygnet.

Madame Cygnet teaches boxing? I shrugged. It was a funny name for a boxer, but maybe it was one of those trick names like the wrestlers on TV.

I tried to imagine what she'd look like as I climbed the stairs. Probably like a body builder with giant muscles that popped out of her arms like watermelons.

She'd probably have beady eyes, a voice like growling tiger and spiky hair. This could be cool.

Or not …

At the top of the stairs, I stopped dead. All I could see was a big open space with a shiny floor. Not a boxing ring in sight. Only a slim lady with a long pointy nose who was frowning at us and pointing at her watch.

"You are very late!" she hissed. "Quickly!

The others are already changing!"

Mum's face turned bright red. "I'm sorry, Madame Cygnet."

This was Madame Cygnet? Where were the watermelon muscles? The spiky hair?

Madame Cygnet's hair was pulled tight into a lump at the back of her head. She turned to stare at me then. Okay—I did get the beady eyes right. They were piercing, like darts.

"Quickly! To the dressing room at once!" she ordered.

Taking the parcel from Mum, I followed the direction of Madame Cygnet's finger and headed to a room with a little man painted on the door. It was totally empty so I found a bench and tore open the parcel wrapping.

And froze.

Shaking my head, I pulled out the garment and shook it. Then I dragged out the shoes...

No way.

NO WAY!

Through my shock I heard Mum's voice through the door. "Matthew? Are you ready? They're waiting."

"I'm not doing it!" I called back. "You can't make me!"

Mum's voice dropped lower, but I could still hear her. "That's okay. You can come out then."

I could? My heart lifted with hope and I started to move towards the door.

Then she began speaking again. "Of course, that means you have to forfeit your cricket gear, your skateboard, your hockey gear, your basketball…"

"My basketball? Not my ball signed by the Jets?"

"The very one." And don't ask me how, but I knew Mum was smiling. That scary one she'd been wearing all morning. And that's also when I knew I couldn't get out of this.

I took a deep breath and dragged myself back to the bench and started getting dressed.

I thought about Henry at school who did classes like this, which made me feel a bit better.

He was super fit and popular with the girls. But this just wasn't my thing.

Just the thought of it was bad enough. This could be the worst day of **doom** yet.

Chapter 4

One, Two, Three, Four, Ple-ay

When I came out, everyone was waiting. By everyone, I mean girls. Heaps of them. All dressed in tutus and ballet shoes. Where were the guys?

Yes, that's right, ballet. My mother had signed me up for ballet. And I was wearing tights. Tights!

How could she do this to me? Her only son.

Mum was smiling. This time it was her nice smile, but it didn't make me feel any better.

"You look fine—actually, you look really cute in those tights. I think you'll be good at this, sweetheart. You're fit and active. And it will be good for you to find something else in life other than soccer, hockey and crick—"

Across the room, Madame clapped her hands and Mum stopped. "You are making us wait, young man! You will hurry! Take a place by the barre and assume the same position as the dancers around you."

Ba? Oh, bar! With a sigh, I walked over and grabbed a rail, which I assumed was the barre. After a quick look at the girl in front of me, I poked both feet out almost sideways and nearly fell over. This ballet thing was harder than it looked!

"I want to see arms, Matthew!" Madame screeched.

Confused, I looked back at her. "I've got arms!" I called back.

"Don't be insolent, young man. Hold them up! Like this."

All around me, the others stood as stiff as soldiers, but Madame still scowled. What was this? Torture? Maybe it was, because suddenly she whacked her long stick against the floor. It cracked through the air like a whip. I figured it was like a referee's whistle. It had the same effect.

Suddenly, music filled the air and Madame screeched again. She was giving instructions and everyone started bobbing up and down. Struggling to hear, I leant forward to hear her say, "One, two, three, four, ple-ay."

One, two, three, four, play? We could play? Play what? Madame was still shouting, and the girl behind me kicked her leg high. It hit me right on the butt! I suddenly got it! This was just a warm-up! A time to muck around and get ready for the main event. Madame wasn't such a grouch after all.

This wasn't so bad. I grinned and turned to the girl with the good left foot. "I get it now! And hey, you kick really well. Want to play soccer in the warm-up?"

The girl frowned, but she was probably wondering what we'd use for a ball.

One glance around the room and I had it covered. There was a ball sitting beside some bags in the corner. Someone must have brought it along so we could play in the warm-ups. I took off, rounding behind it so I could hook it to the side to try it out.

Big mistake! That ball seemed to be made of lead!

Worse! I'd forgotten I was wearing the ballet slipper things. "Ouch!" I yelled and dropped to the floor holding my toe.

Behind me, I heard Madame yell.

"It's okay," I called back. "I don't think it's broken. I'll be okay."

Then she was in front of me. "You foolish boy! I don't care about your toe! You've ruined my lunch!"

"W … what?"

"Look at what you've done!" she screeched.

I did and my heart sank. My kick was better than I thought. Even though the ball was so heavy, I'd lifted it right up to a small table in the corner. And that's where it had landed. Right on a plate of salad that was now splattered up the walls.

Beetroot juice ran like rivers of blood, shredded lettuce lay across the table and floor. Grated carrot was scattered like orange grass clippings and boiled egg hung off all surfaces like it had been shot out of a cannon. I gulped and darted a look at Madame Cygnet. And I suddenly experienced real fear.

"You are clearly not meant to be a ballet dancer. Go back to your football or your soccer. Please leave immediately!" she ordered.

As I was dragged out, for the first time all morning, Mum wasn't smiling. In fact, I was pretty sure there was steam coming out of her ears. And nose.

As she dragged me away, I tried to explain. "But Mum, it wasn't my fault. She said to play! I thought it was like a warm-up session!"

"That's *plié*, Matthew. Pli-é!" she answered in a really tight voice. "It's French; it means to bend your knees!"

"But they had a ball there. Except it was the weirdest kind of ball . . ."

"For your information that was a medicine ball! They use it for balance exercises! Not for soccer!"

Chapter 5 

Back To Your Room

Back at home, I was sent to my room while my parents talked. Trust me, nothing good could come out of that talk. At least they fed me though. The way Mum had been carrying on, I'd expected stale bread and water. For a year.

The only bright spot in my day was when my mate Aydin arrived for dinner. I think with all the drama, Mum forgot. So when Aydin turned up, she couldn't exactly tell him dinner was off. I still wasn't allowed to watch TV and in truth, I wasn't great company, so it didn't take long for Aydin to get bored. He started hunting around in my wardrobe. "Hey! What's this?"

I looked at the box he held up. "I don't know. Some electronics thing. My uncle gave it to me for Christmas."

"This is so cool!" he yelled. "Why haven't you used it?"

I shrugged. "I've been too busy."

"Doing what?"

I sighed and told him about my **doomed** life. I expected sympathy, but he just shrugged. "Henry does ballet."

"I know that. Ballet is actually really, really hard," I answered, gingerly wriggling my sore toe. "But I'm sticking to sports."

"Ballet *is* a sport, man!"

"Really? Okay then, I'm sticking to easier sports!"

Aydin chuckled. "It was probably a good thing you were so bad at ballet. What do you suppose your parents are planning next? Knitting?"

He laughed, but to me it wasn't funny. For all I knew, that's exactly what they were planning.

"Hey, can I open this?" Aydin asked, pointing to the box. I nodded.

Aydin tore into the box, oohing and ahhing every time he pulled out something new. He was so excited that when Dad came to call us for dinner, he asked if we could eat in my room.

Frowning, I sat down on the floor beside him. "You're acting a bit freaky over this game," I told him.

"It's not a game, Matt. Do you know what this stuff can do?"

He shoved the manual under my nose, but I just shrugged. "No idea. I've never even looked at it."

He looked back at me in amazement. "How could you do that? Look! You can make all kinds of cool things!"

I yawned. "Like what?"

"Like electronic surveillance gear for starters."

My eyes popped. "Electr—what?"

Aydin sighed. "That's spy stuff to you..."

Suddenly, I perked up as a lightbulb flashed in my head. "Real spy stuff?" When he nodded, I laughed. "Aydin my man, you have just saved my life!"

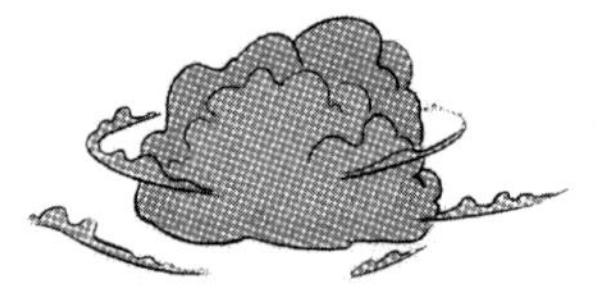

Chapter 6 

Spies 'R' Us

"How have I saved your life?" he asked.

I grinned. "I figure all I have to do is be really, really bad at everything my parents suggest, right? That way, they'll have to give in and realise that the only thing I'm good at is sport!"

Aydin frowned. "So tell me again, how did I save your life?"

"The electronics set! Do you reckon you could teach me to build a listening bug so I can hear what people are saying?"

It took a while, but we finally worked out how to create a recording device that we could listen to right here in my room.

Once that was done, we had to work out how to "plant" it so that my parents didn't notice. I had the most brilliant idea—I fitted it into my old remote-controlled car, and then I sent it down to where Mum and Dad sat drinking coffee in the living room.

Then all we had to do was sit back and listen.

Most of it was boring stuff about bills and then about the cost of repairing the TV. I felt bad about that, but I scowled when I heard that my little sister had aced her last spelling test. Aydin laughed at me.

Finally, they got to the subject I was most interested in—me.

"Macramé," I heard Mum say.

"His first lesson is Tuesday?" Dad asked.

"Yep," Mum answered.

Macramé. What on earth was macramé? I wondered. Suddenly, my plan was deflating faster than a burst balloon. How could I be prepared if I didn't even know what it was?

"I'm even more **doomed**," I moaned.

"Internet?" Aydin suggested.

I shook my head. "I'm banned."

Aydin sighed. "You're right. You're doomed." Then he paused. "Or maybe not. I think I have a plan…"

Chapter 7

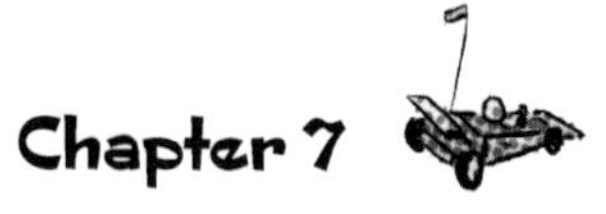

Tied in Knots

On Monday morning, Aydin was waiting for me at school as usual. "The library's open, let's go and see if we can check out this macramé stuff before the bell rings."

When we asked Mr Pike, the librarian, he smiled. "The best way to learn is to research for yourselves. You know where the computers are, and you could have a look at some books in the second aisle."

"Great, thanks," I mumbled.

We found it—macramé was making things with knots! No kidding! You take some bits of string or wool or something, and you knot them together to make things. Like bags and stuff.

"Why would anyone want to do that?" Aydin muttered.

I flicked through a few pages. "Actually, there's some really cool stuff here. Like that huge boat that you could hang from the ceiling." I screwed up my face. "But still, I don't think it's what I want to do."

The planning part came next. "You'll need heavy string," Aydin offered.

"No problem," I said, giving him a high five. On the way out of the library, we passed the sports section. "Hey! Here's a book on the Socceroos!"

Mr Pike heard me. "You can borrow it if you like, Matthew."

I nodded. "Well, Mum didn't say anything about being banned from reading about sport."

That evening, I was sitting in the living room with a ball of string.

I started to try to make something, but within minutes I had a huge messy tangle spread all over the room. Somehow, I'd really and truly made a mess, a bigger mess than I'd meant to. String was strung from one chair to another. It was a **disaster** waiting to happen.

And then it did...

Mum and Dad wandered in with their coffee. "What are you doing?" asked Dad.

"Oh, just this thing I read about at school," I answered.

Dad came closer. Before I knew it, he caught his foot on the string and went sprawling across the floor. I hadn't meant for that to happen!

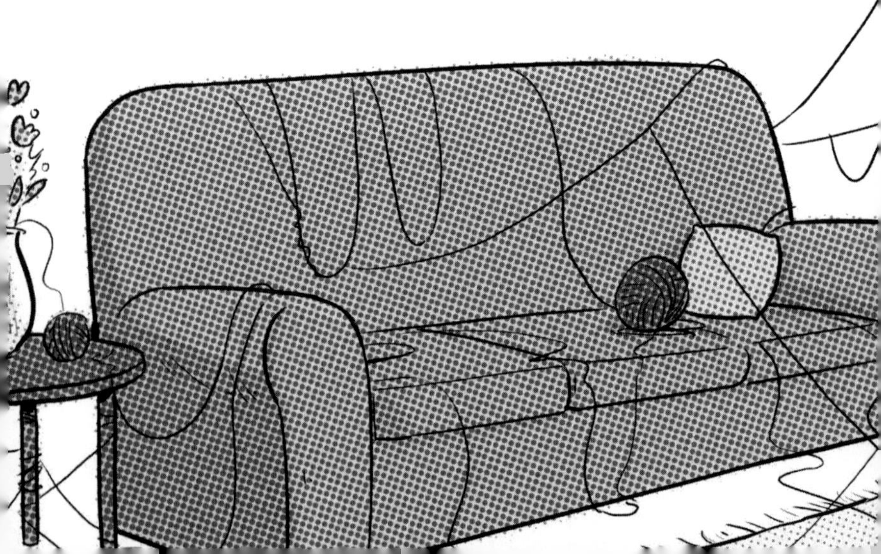

"I'm really sorry Dad! Are you hurt?"

I rushed over, but somehow my foot got caught as well, and I skidded across the floor, landing on top of Dad. There was a **crash** and then an **oompf**!

Dad looked at me in disbelief. His "I ♥ My Family" mug was in a million pieces. Biscuit crumbs stuck to his nose. "You're grounded until you're 100, Matthew! And one more thing—I'm giving away our season pass to the Jets!" he yelled.

Our season pass! This was bad; the worst! The cloud of **doom** was so thick now I could hardly see. I staggered back to my room. I felt about as low as low. My toe and now my knee throbbed. Then I remembered the bugged remote-controlled car and sent it into the living room.

"Looks like macramé mightn't be the thing for Matt," Mum said. "But, what about the mandolin? That could work!"

My heart sank. Mandolin? What was that? Did I even want to find out? But if I didn't then I'd never be able to play basketball again! Or cricket. Or soccer.

I sighed. Library, here we come. Again.

At least I had my Socceroos book to read.

At school the next morning, I had one word for Aydin. "Mandolin."

In the library, it didn't take us long to discover that it was a musical instrument. In fact, it was a cross between a guitar, a violin and a banjo. Wild! Part of me was a bit confused because it probably would be quite cool to play.

But I had to stick to the plan to get back to sport as soon as I could. The thing was, how could I prove to Mum that the mandolin wasn't for me?

"I know," said Aydin. "You can borrow my brother's old electric guitar."

"How will that work?"

Aydin smiled. "When they hear you try to play it, it's got to make them realise that music isn't your thing."

"At least I can't injure myself with it," I muttered.

On the way out, Mr Pike waved me over. "How's the Socceroos book, Matt?"

"It's really great!"

He smiled. "Good, good." But as I turned, I noticed another book on his desk. It was on electronics. I started flicking through it. "You can borrow it too, if you like," he offered.

Later that evening, I put the latest plan into action. Within minutes, Mum was at the door. She looked cross, and she had her hands over her ears. "What is that awful noise?"

I shrugged. "I just borrowed this old guitar. Cool, huh? Do you reckon I could start a band? I've been writing a song. Listen."

Mum pressed her ears harder. "Cool? It sounds like ten cats with their tails caught under a rocking chair! Next door's dog has run away!"

"So, does that mean you'd like me to stop?" I asked innocently.

When Mum sighed and nodded, I made just one final enthusiastic twang. Trouble was, I twanged just a bit too enthusiastically and the metal string shot out and flicked my hand! "Ooouch!" I yelled. "Oh man! That's worse than a bee sting!"

I put the guitar away, and while I got ready for bed, I sent the remote control car back into the living room.

Chapter 8 

"Master Chef", Here I Come...

"**Gourmet cuisine!** You'd think they'd come up with something I don't have to look up!" I grumbled to Aydin the next day as we made our way straight to the library.

Mr Pike greeted us with a huge smile. "What is it today, boys?"

When we told him, he pointed to the computer. "By the way, Matthew, how did you enjoy the electronics book?"

"It's totally cool, Mr Pike! Yesterday arvo, I used it to make a new invention! I made our kitchen bin give a little squeal when it's full!"

Aydin frowned. "Couldn't you tell just by looking at it?"

I shrugged and shuffled my feet. "I s'pose. But this way no-one can ignore it because the squeal won't stop till someone empties it!"

At least Mr Pike was impressed. "I think it's brilliant."

I couldn't stop grinning.

"I'm sure my wife and I would like one of those!" he continued.

"Yeah?" I beamed some more. "Well, maybe I could make you one too! I've got heaps of stuff in my electronics kit."

I handed over the soccer book.

Gourmet cuisine turned out to be cooking. Now that one was a no-brainer. I didn't even have to pretend—I was the worst at cooking.

Before we left the library, I took one more peek around the sports section and found a book called *The Greatest Sport of All.*

Aydin was right behind me. "It's about chess; you ever played?"

I shook my head. "Is it really a sport?"

Aydin nodded. "The top players train for years, and they play in competitions all over the world."

"All over the world, huh?" Without even thinking, I walked to Mr Pike's desk with the chess book. It wouldn't hurt to look at it. Better than sitting around without TV.

That evening, I waited till everyone was home before proving that I wasn't very good in the kitchen. "Anyone feel like a snack?" I asked in a loud voice.

No-one jumped in. "Okay, I think I'll just make myself some toast."

There are some things you need to know about toasting. One of them is not to lean over the toaster waiting for it to pop. I knew that, but the toast popped up really fast and hit me fair and square on the nose! It didn't hurt, but in my surprise, I jerked my head up hard and whacked it on the cupboard above!

I saw stars for a full minute, and the lump on my skull was the size of an egg! This had to stop! I never had this many injuries playing sport.

After the toast episode, Mum and Dad decided that I would be safer out of the kitchen, but I did hear Mum mention art. At least I didn't have to look that up.

Still, I was feeling pretty sore and sorry for myself when I climbed into bed with my new chess book, but it really hooked me in. And it was only when I was drifting off to sleep that I remembered...

Tomorrow was my birthday.

How could I have forgotten that!

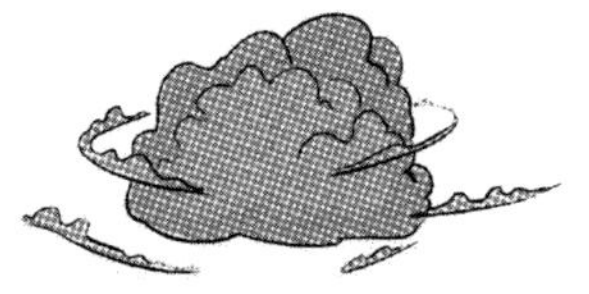

Chapter 9

Quack!

"Happy birthday Matthew!" Mum and Dad chorused. Mum leant down to wake me with a kiss, and Dad handed me a plate of bacon and toast. After yesterday, I wasn't sure I wanted to see a piece of toast ever again.

"Thanks," I said sleepily.

Mum ruffled my hair. I winced and felt the lump on my head. "You'll get your presents later tonight. The ban on TV is lifted for the day," she said, "but it starts again tomorrow."

"And don't forget the special birthday dinner tonight!" Dad added with a grin. "The whole family is coming over! Best behaviour, okay?"

I had to hand it to my parents, they didn't give up easily. Tomorrow, the torture would start all over again. That meant I had to stay one step ahead of them.

Maybe if I showed them how bad I was at art in front of the whole family, someone (like Grandma) might jump in to talk some sense into my parents. It was a good plan, and I couldn't wait till school ended, so I could put it into practice.

As soon as I got home, I went down to the back shed. No-one ever used it anymore, but it was filled with old junk that might help me.

The search didn't take long. I found a tin of gross pink paint, probably left over from my sister's room. Perfect. Trouble was, the lid was stuck down tight.

I thumped against it, shook it, and then tried to lift it with the claw of a hammer. Nothing moved that lid.

Frustrated, I searched and found an old screwdriver. Placing the paint can between my knees, I jammed the sharp edge of the screwdriver under the lid.

"Come on..." I coaxed. It was a bad move.

All of a sudden it came loose! But the momentum had thrown me backwards, and the can tipped upside down and I was covered in stinky, sticky pink paint!

"Ahhh!" I yelled, still falling backwards. My arms flung helplessly in front of me trying to find something to grab. My back landed against something hard.

It was an old shelf. An old shelf that held more cans of paint. Cans whose lids weren't on so tight! "No! No!" A rainbow of coloured paint poured over me.

Closing my eyes tightly, I focused on keeping my balance and shutting my mouth. But I tilted left, then right—finally falling sideways and hoping for a soft landing.

It was. Thank goodness! And only then did I realise I was covered in feathers. And I mean covered! From head to toe. Feathers that had come out of an old, torn feather quilt that was waiting to be thrown out.

Finally on my feet, but barely able to see, I struggled to the door and headed towards the house and the bathroom. I made it to the back door without anyone seeing me, checked that the coast was clear, and raced inside.

Unfortunately, wet paint and slippery tiles don't mix! I felt myself skidding and skating towards the living room. Laughter followed me.

Lots of laughter. Realisation hit—my relatives! My whole family had arrived for my birthday dinner. Early!

And what did they get? Me, covered in paint and feathers! A rainbow-coloured duck!

"It's the duck of **doom**," my sister snorted.

"I didn't know we were having duck for dinner," Grandpa joked.

I ignored them. Only two faces caught my eye. My parents. "I give up," I croaked. "You win. I'll do whatever you want."

Dad was laughing too. "Mate, we didn't want to win. We just wanted you to have some interests other than sport."

"But it didn't work. I still didn't get any new interests."

HAPPY BIRTHDAY

"Didn't you?" Dad asked with a grin. "What about all those books?"

"And electronics. And maybe even chess!" Mum added with a funny twinkle in her eye. "See? We've been paying attention!"

The funny twinkle bothered me. And then I knew. I smacked my hand against my forehead, spraying paint around the room. "You knew, didn't you! You knew I was listening!"

My parents couldn't hold back their laughter for one more minute. "We guessed the first day! That surveillance bug is a two-way radio! You could hear us—but we could also hear you!" Dad explained.

I groaned.

Mum was bent over laughing. "Macramé was the funniest! You were in such a mess!"

Dad started laughing too. "It would have been even funnier if it wasn't so painful."

"Okay," I admitted with a grin. "You outsmarted me. And okay, yes, I did learn some things. I mean, some of that stuff really is cool! Especially the electronics." That reminded me. "Just wait! I want to show you something!"

In seconds I was back. "Watch this! It's this new thing I've been working on. It can throw a ball—you just push this button here and then twiddle this knob. So I'll be able to play cricket and handball by myself. I haven't quite worked it all out yet, but—"

The crashing noise echoed through the whole house. And probably next door as well. Or maybe that was Mum's groan and Dad's gasp.

"Oops! Sorry. You can take all my pocket money. And take back my birthday presents. I won't ask for anything, I promise. Not until the window is paid for."

They both stared at me—their mouths wide open. I sighed. I knew that look.

It's true—my life is doomed. Totally **doomed**.